SOUNDS AMAZING

Ray Plays all Day

play in the spray

On Mondays in May,

Ray likes to play

In the deep of the bay,

Far, far away.

He may play all day,

As he knows his way.

A swish and a sway

In the froth of the spray.

Whale Makes a Mistake

I hate waves

Whale is not very brave,

She feels sea-sick at every big wave.

She does not behave as a whale

In even a very small gale.

"Of course, it's the waves that I hate,

I think I shall have to migrate."

She swims to a very nice place,

But where, oh where was the space?

Had Whale made a mighty mistake

To move to a tiny, round lake?

Snail in the Rain

snail wails in pain

Along her daily daisy trail

On the thin rim of a pail,

Gail the snail lets out a wail

As she slips and bumps her tail.

She is in a bit of pain,

Though it really is quite plain,

For a snail with little brain,

That her slip was due to rain.

Cheeky Parakeet

tweet, tweet, tweet

"Tweet, tweet, tweet,"

Screeched Green Parakeet

As he greedily gobbled three seeds.

The chimpanzee queen,

Who was only sixteen,

Went as white as a sheet to her knees.

"What a cheek!" she decreed

At his terrible greed,

And she chased him right out of her tree.

Flea has a Feast

seal squeals

Flea hops onto Seal

As Seal sits on the beach.

Seal lets out a squeal

As Flea is out of reach.

Seal is not too pleased

To be Flea's midday meal.

Fed up with the flea,

He heaves back to sea.

"Oh dear!" squeaks the flea,

"I should finish my feast.

I can't breathe in the sea"

And she jumps from that beast.

Kitty is the Cat from the City

kitty is dizzy

Kitty is the cat from the city.

In springtime she really is dizzy.

When it's drizzly she drones, "What a pity."

When it's cloudy she thinks, "It is dowdy!"

When it's frosty her fur gets all frizzy.

When it's windy she is jolly silly,

And when it is sunny

She just feels so funny.

Kitty is the cat from the city.

In springtime she really is dizzy.

Knight has a Fright

fright at night

In the dead of the night

A bat took flight

To frighten a knight

In the bright moonlight.

The bat was delighted

To frighten fortnightly,

A knight who thought he was

So high and mighty.

The short-sighted knight,

Thighs wobbling with fright,

Sighed at his plight

In the dead of the night.

A Nice Crocodile

smile and slide

With her ice white smile,

She smiles for a while,

As Caroline is quite

A nice crocodile.

So she hides in the slime

On the side of the Nile

Where she slides around

Mile after mile after mile.

She doesn't think twice

When she dines on mice.

She thinks they're quite nice

With hot spice and rice.

Shy Butterfly

fly in the sky

The shy butterfly sat in the sty
With her friend, the fly, flying nearby.

"I don't mean to pry," said the low flying fly
As he flew by the poor butterfly,

"But why, oh why, can't you fly in the sky?
Give it a try, it's July and it's dry."

"I don't know why I am so shy!"
Was her reply as she started to cry.

"You have style," said the fly, "don't hide in the sty.
Come with me and fly into the sky."

Fried Pie

magpie cried and cried

Magpie cried and cried
As his mince pie was deep-fried.
He always tried and tried
To eat his pie sun-dried.

A Row in the Snow

row in the snow

Sparrow did not know

That Crow liked to row,

Even in the snow

When the wind did blow.

The water was very shallow

And really rather narrow

But Crow rowed straight as an arrow

To see his good friend Sparrow.

Mole all Alone

mole broke a bone

As Mole was accident-prone,

He stayed at home in his dome.

But as he spoke on the phone,

He tripped and fell on a stone.

He broke the bone in his nose,

Down in his hole all alone.

Toad on a Boat

toad has a croak

On a little boat

Around the rocky coast

Toad didn't zip his coat

And he didn't wear his cloak

So now the frog in his throat

Makes him croak, croak, croak.

Goose on the Loose

swoop and whoop

"I'm flying to the Moon,"

Said Goose, "At noon."

"Can I come too?"

Asked Cockatoo with a coo.

"Can I come too?"

Requested Coot with a toot.

"Can I come too?"

Demanded Moose with a moo.

"Can I come too?"

Inquired Baboon with a croon.

From the schoolroom at noon

They climbed on the broom.

With a swoop and a whoop

They looped the loop,

All the way to the Moon.

Shrewd Old Shrew

chew and chew on stew

Shrew's teeth were so few

And not so very new.

However shrewd the old shrew grew

He knew, with stew, he had to chew.

Bluebottles are Blue

it is true

It is true that bluebottles are blue

But it's not true that they like to queue.

With the whiff of a barbecue,

At the end of The Avenue,

Bluebottles do not have a clue

How to form an orderly queue.

In the Nook of a Wood

a good book

Rook took a look

At a very good book

In the nook of a wood

Where an oak tree stood.

He understood from his book

How to fish with a hook.

With a worm and some wool,

That's all it took.

The powerful Bull

push and pull

Abdul is a powerful bull.

He eats bushes in one mouthful.

The farmer tries to push

The bull from his beautiful bush

And Abdul tries to pull

To stay put until he is full.

Cute Mule

use the flute

Mule plays a magical tune

Amongst the dunes in June.

She uses her flute to amuse the Duke,

Who also likes her perfume.

Hound on the Scrounge

our hound

Our hound loves to scrounge

Around on the ground

For sprouts that roll around and about.

When our hound found a sprout

He sniffed with his snout

And with a pounce he proudly devoured it.

Brown Cow the Clown

wow wow wow

Dressed as a clown,
Down in the town,
Brown Cow bows
In front of the crowd.
"Me-ow," mews the cow
And the crowd howls "Wow!"

Royal Oyster

land ahoy land ahoy

Oyster is a Royal

And his followers are loyal.

But boy oh boy does he annoy

Roy, the boy, in his convoy

When Oyster shouts out in his joy,

"Land ahoy, land ahoy!"

Droid from the Void

oi I need oil

Droid flew in on an asteroid

From a void in outer space.

"Oi!" said the droid

From the extra-terrestrial void

As he fell into moist soil,

Where he thought his coils would spoil.

"I think my joints are noisy

And the points may need some oil."